You shouldn't have to prove
your worth as a person.

But Joseph Pierce had to.

Not once,

not twice,

but countless times.

His story began in China.

He had another name then,
but he wasn't considered important
enough for anyone to remember it.

Few people remember the name
Joseph Pierce now.

Maybe you will.

by ANDREA WANG

Illustrated by YOUA VANG

LEVINE QUERIDO

Montclair | Amsterdam | Hoboken

WORTHY

The Brave and Capable Life of
Joseph Pierce

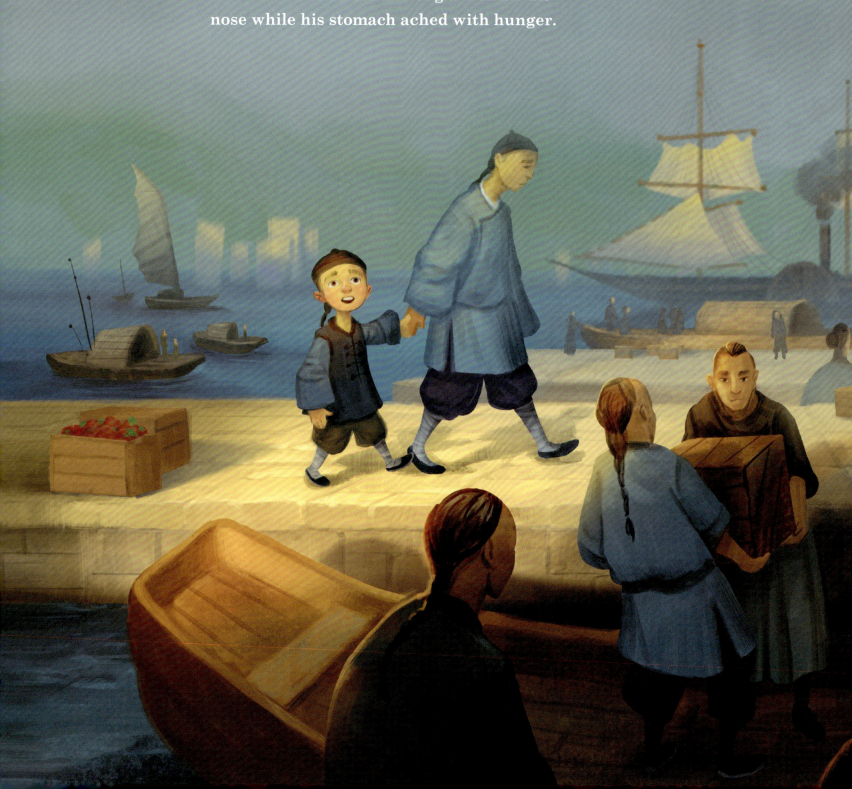

One damp, gray day,

he trotted behind his father on
Canton's noisy, bustling wharf.

The aromas of coffee and sugar tickled his
nose while his stomach ached with hunger.

The rice jar at home had been empty for days. Maybe there would be food today.

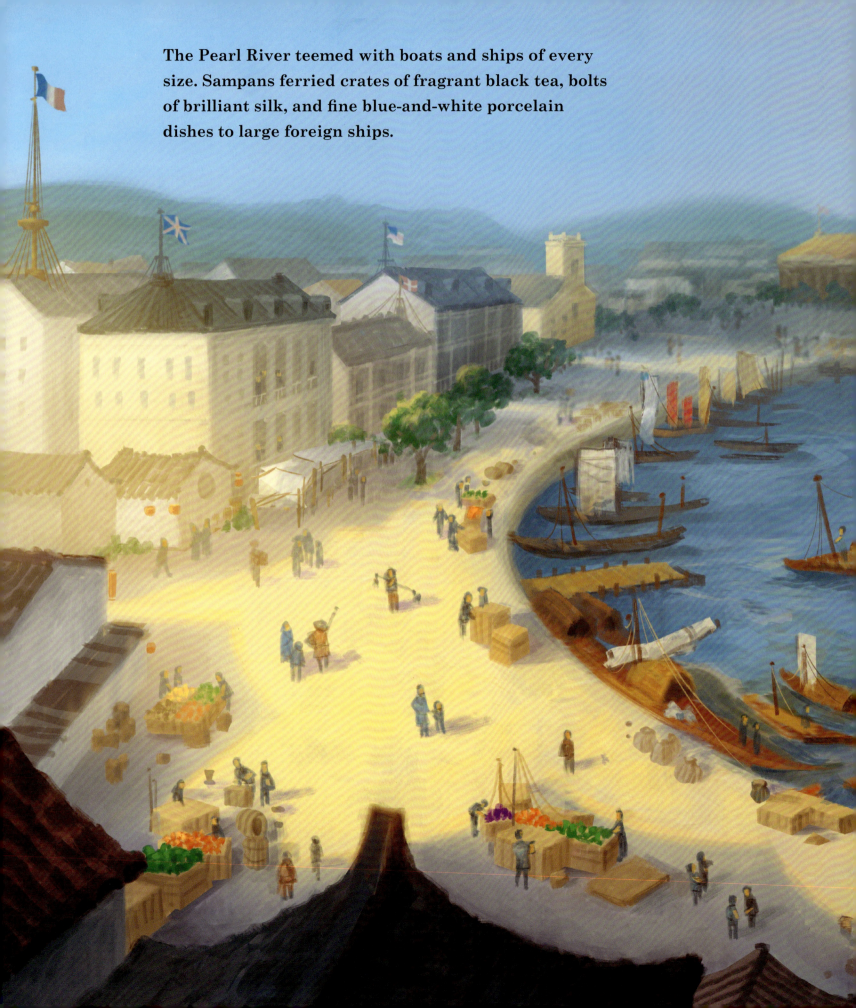

The Pearl River teemed with boats and ships of every size. Sampans ferried crates of fragrant black tea, bolts of brilliant silk, and fine blue-and-white porcelain dishes to large foreign ships.

White men sneered down from the windows of enormous factories. Above them, giant flags furled and unfurled like the greedy mouths of fish.

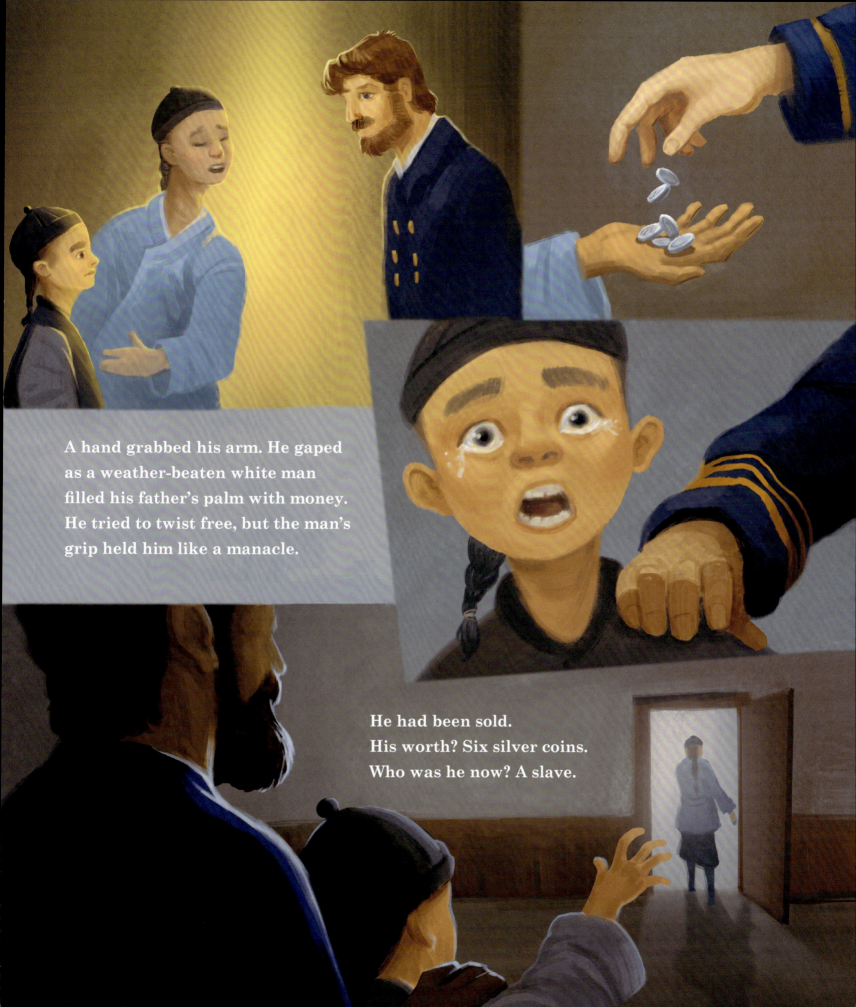

A hand grabbed his arm. He gaped as a weather-beaten white man filled his father's palm with money. He tried to twist free, but the man's grip held him like a manacle.

He had been sold.
His worth? Six silver coins.
Who was he now? A slave.

He had nothing. No home. No family. No language. Not even his name. The waves had swept away everything he had ever known.

Canton faded into the mist as he wondered what lay ahead for him.

Captain Peck and the crew called him "Joe."

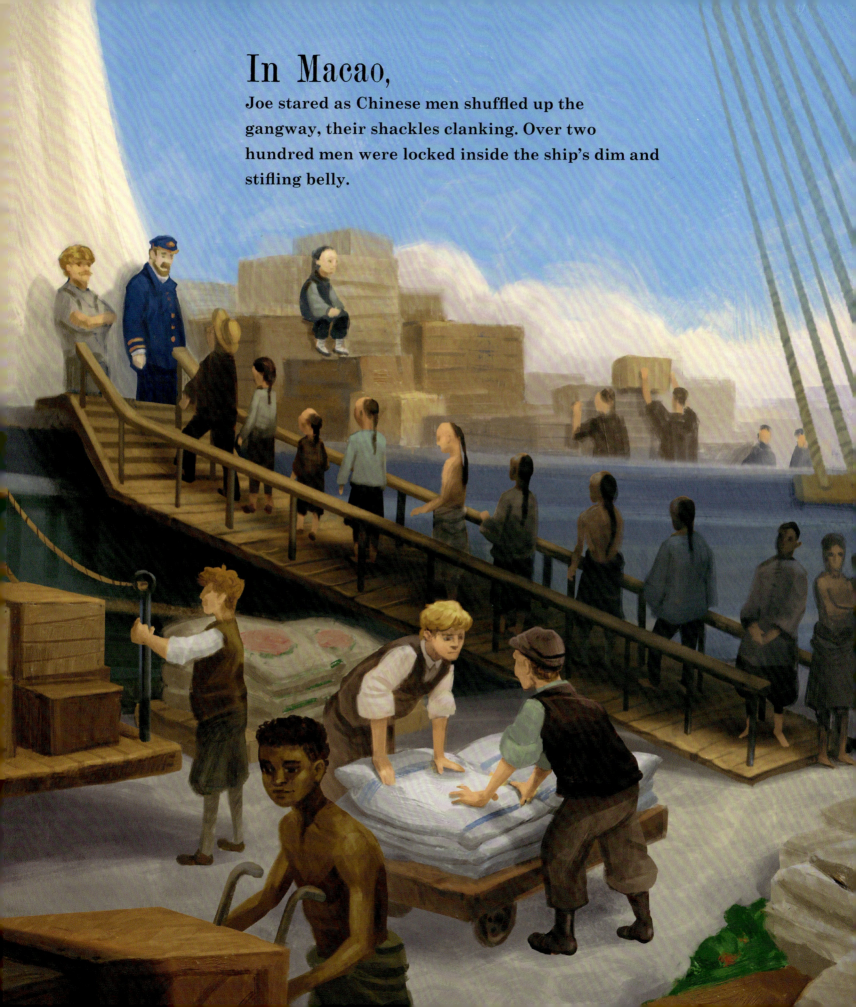

In Macao,

Joe stared as Chinese men shuffled up the gangway, their shackles clanking. Over two hundred men were locked inside the ship's dim and stifling belly.

Joe listened as the prisoners shared their stories.
Some had signed contracts. Others had been tricked.
Many had been kidnapped. All were being sent to
work on the sugar plantations of Cuba.

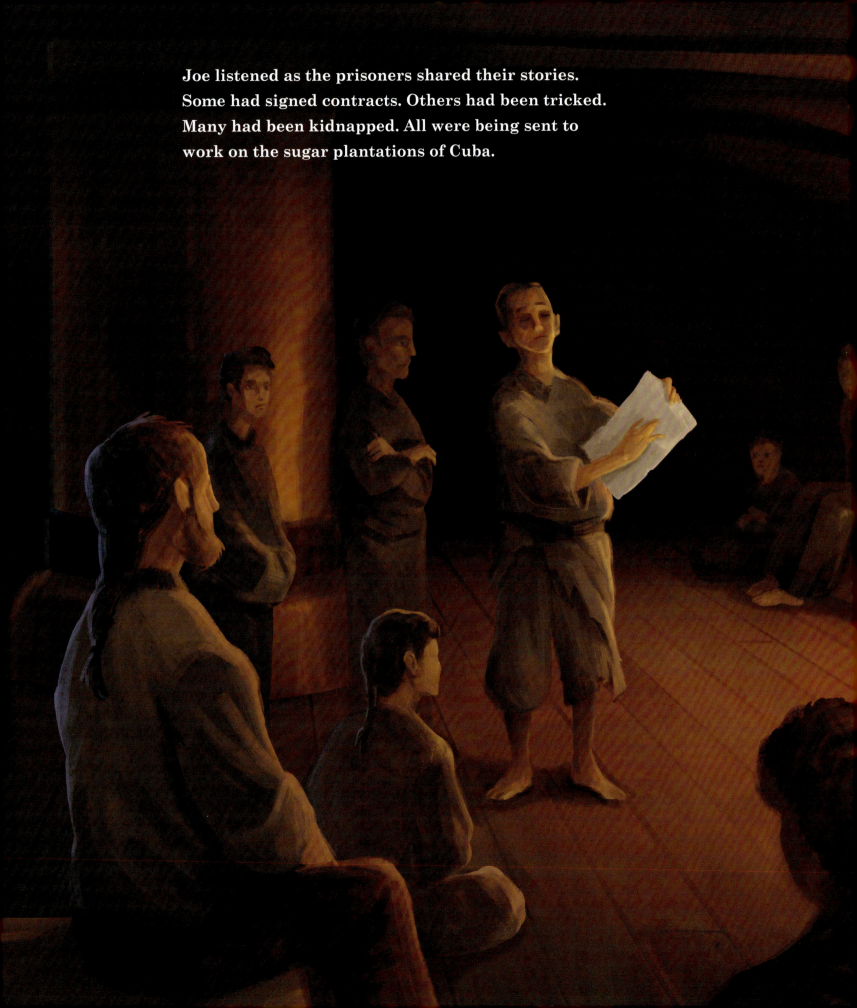

Poor and starving, they had lost
their freedom. Just like Joe.

Maybe he was
headed to Cuba, too.

Months passed as *The Hound* sailed through storms and sunrises.

Joe was put to work helping the cook,

delivering messages,
and serving the
officers and crew.

He tried to prove that he could
do more than cut sugarcane.

In Havana,

Joe's heart thumped as the Chinese laborers hobbled to the market.

White men wielding whips drove
other groups of Chinese workers
across the pier.

Some of them looked
as young as Joe.

Was he going to be sold again?

When the crew hoisted the sails, Joe was still on board. Relieved, he wondered if he would be a cabin boy forever.

Was that all he was worth?

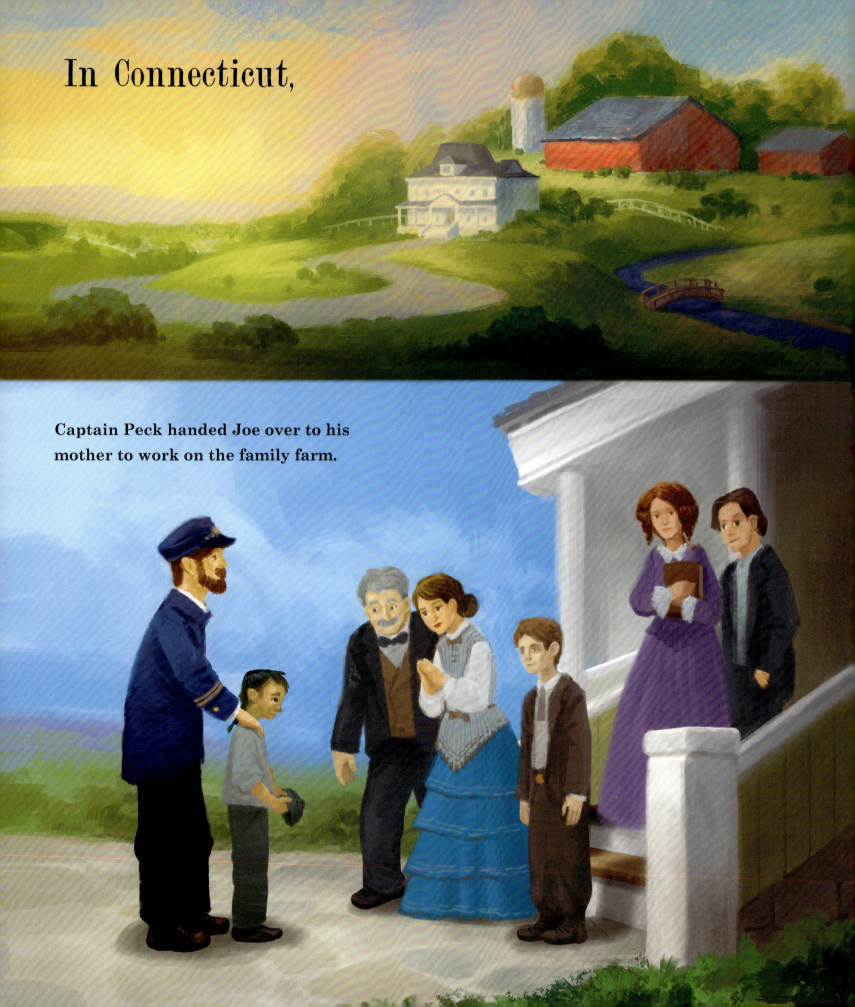

In Connecticut,

Captain Peck handed Joe over to his mother to work on the family farm.

The Pecks renamed him

Joseph Pierce.

Although slavery had been
outlawed in Connecticut,
Joe was still a child.
He had no money.
He had nowhere to go.

The Pecks treated him like a member of the family. Almost. Most Americans had never seen a Chinese person before.

What they knew came from newspaper articles—

"The Chinese are ignorant and insolent."
—THE NEW YORK TIMES, OCTOBER 2, 1852

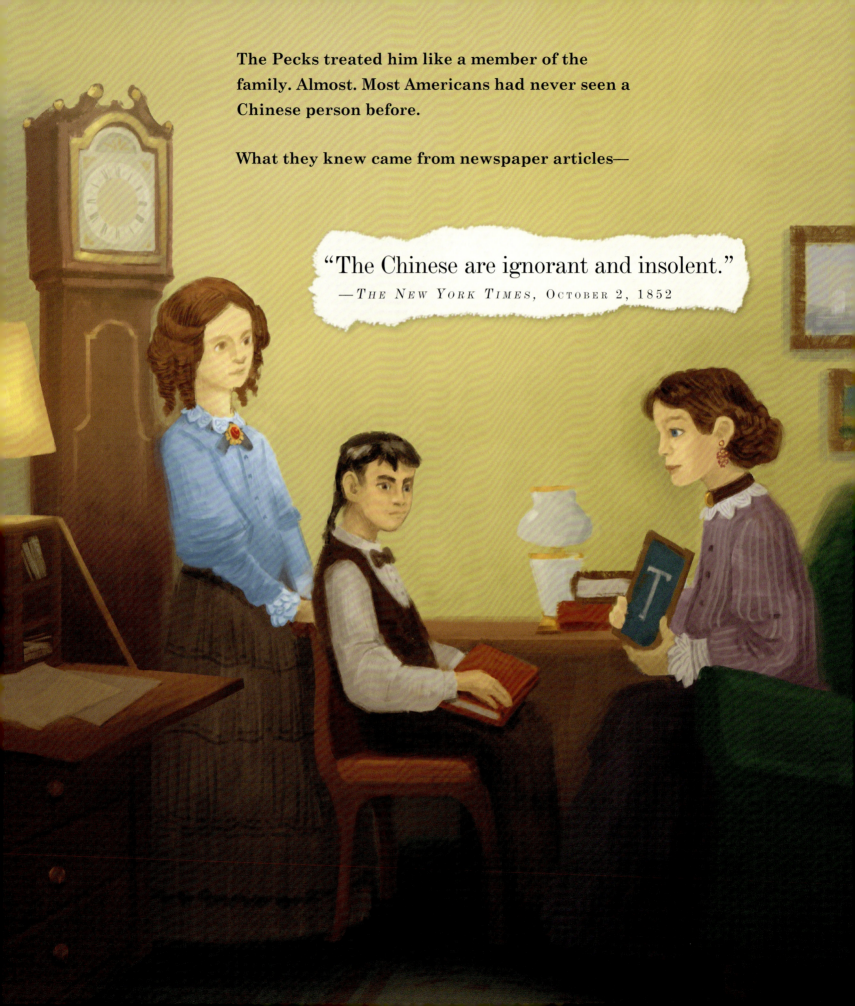

Joe sat up straight. He had carried messages between the crew. Now, he went to school with the Peck children and learned to read and write English, his second language. He studied arithmetic, history, and geography.

"They will not work unless treated...as slaves. They cannot be so treated here, and there would therefore be no remedy for their laziness."

—THE NEW YORK TIMES, MAY 28, 1855

Joe squared his shoulders. He had run errands on the ship. Now, from sunup to sundown, he chopped wood, cleaned the barn, and tended the animals.

He plowed,

planted, and weeded.

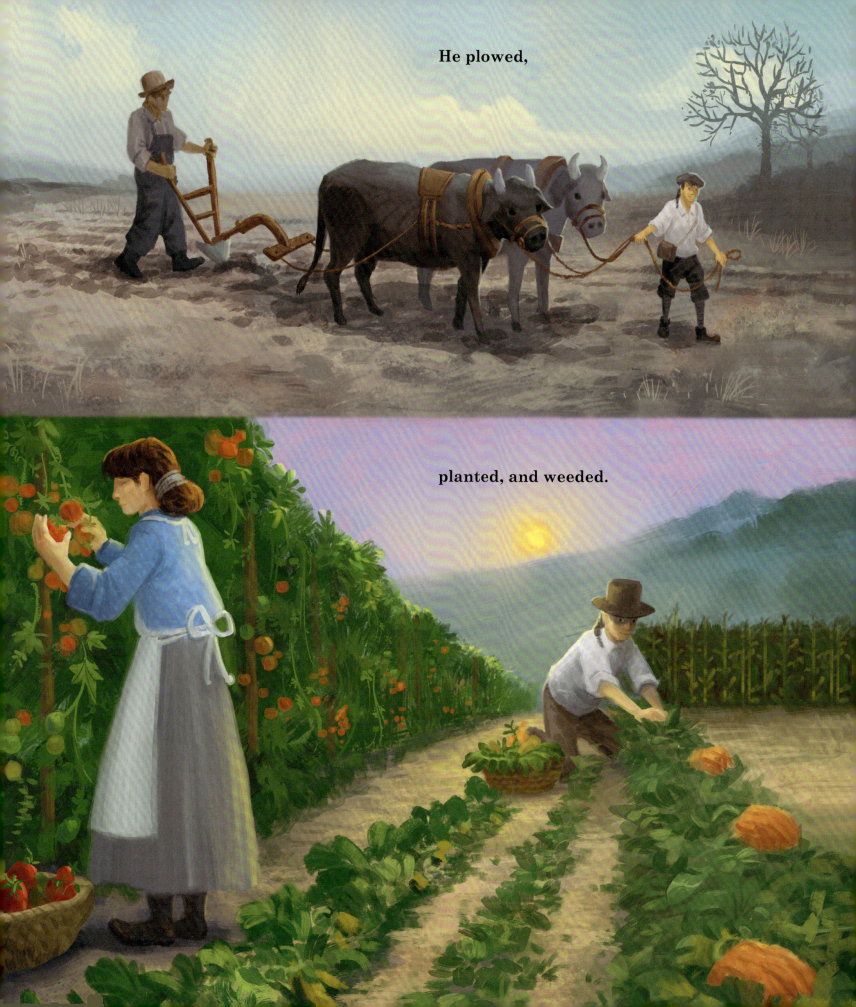

"The Chinese of California celebrated May-day in a high old style. Among the dishes prepared...was a pot-pie, made of...one door mat, two cats, three pair of boots, one dog, four poll parrots, one pair of cotton socks, sixteen snapping turtles, and the fore quarter of a horse." — THE HARTFORD COURANT, AUGUST 24, 1855

Joe rolled his eyes. He had never eaten any of those things.

Homesick, he snuck out one night and made rice and other Chinese dishes over a campfire in the barn.

"None but parents among a heathen, sin-loving people, can know the many difficulties attending the moral instruction of their children while in such close proximity to such a people."

—THE RALEIGH CHRISTIAN ADVOCATE, DECEMBER 22, 1859

Joe shook his head. He had served, obeyed, and respected the Pecks. He knelt in the church pews with them and saw that Christians and Chinese shared many of the same values. Duty and honor lay at the heart of Chinese culture, too.

"Your Chinaman is the most worthless citizen possible."

—The New York Times, May 28, 1855

Joe heaved a sigh. No matter how well he did in school or how hard he worked on the farm, most white people saw him as inferior and called him hateful names. They agreed with *The Daily Alta* that Chinese were "not of our people and never will be."

Joe wondered if he could ever change their minds. How could he prove his worth?

His chance came when Confederate troops opened fire on Fort Sumter. Civil war had begun. Recruitment posters in town stirred Joe's sense of honor and duty.

Now an adult, Joe was still working on the Peck farm.

He wanted more—a home, a family. But people of color couldn't become citizens. And only citizens could vote or own property.

14th Conn. Infantry.
ONE MORE CHANCE TO Serve YOUR COUNTRY!
RALLY! MEN!
RALLY!!

FOR

THE UNION, CONSTITUTION, AND ENFORCEMENT OF THE LAWS.

OUR COUNTRY CALLS FOR MORE MEN!!
CONNECTICUT CALLS for ONE MORE REGIMENT.

Good pay, good rations, good clothing; families provided for; thirty dollars a year bounty from the State; one hundred dollars bounty from the government; competent and deserving men will be promoted, irrespective of rank.

By authority of His Excellency, WM. A. BUCKINGHAM, Commander-in-chief,

JAMES B. COIT,

Late of the Staff of the Second Conn. Regiment Volunteers, has opened

Apollo Hall, Norwich,

To recruit a Company of 100 ABLE BODIED MEN for the

FOURTEENTH CONN. INFANTRY,
Col. Dwight Morris.

COMPENSATION.

$25.00 per MONTH, with CLOTHING and RATIONS, to men having wife and two or more children.
23.50 .... wife and one child.
21.50 .... wife only.
16.50 .... Single.

Families of Volunteers enlisting in this company, draw monthly pay in Norwich. Pay and rations commence at time of enlistment.

For further information, enquire at the

Recruiting Office, Opposite Wauregan House, Norwich, Conn.

Then, Congress passed a law that said anyone born in a foreign country could become a citizen if they served in the United States army.

Nine days later, Joe went to enlist.

The mustering officer rejected Joe. The Union Army didn't accept people of color. *The New York Times* had said that Chinese people made "poor sailors and no soldiers at all."

Joe scoffed. He had already sailed halfway across the world. He could prove his worth as a soldier, too.

Captain Peck, who was now a colonel in the Union Army, vouched for Joe.

The officer said Joe could join up—as a cook. Joe stood firm. "If I can't serve my country as a soldier, I will not remain in the army at all," he said.

Impressed by Joe's will, the officer gave in.

Joe became Private Pierce, the only Chinese soldier in the 14th Regiment of the Connecticut Volunteer Infantry.

Joe's regiment was sent off from Hartford with great fanfare. As crowds cheered and cannons boomed, Joe boarded the steamer ship *City of Hartford*.

Once again, Joe wondered what lay ahead for him.

From the beats of "Reveille" at dawn
to "Tattoo" at dusk, Joe trained.

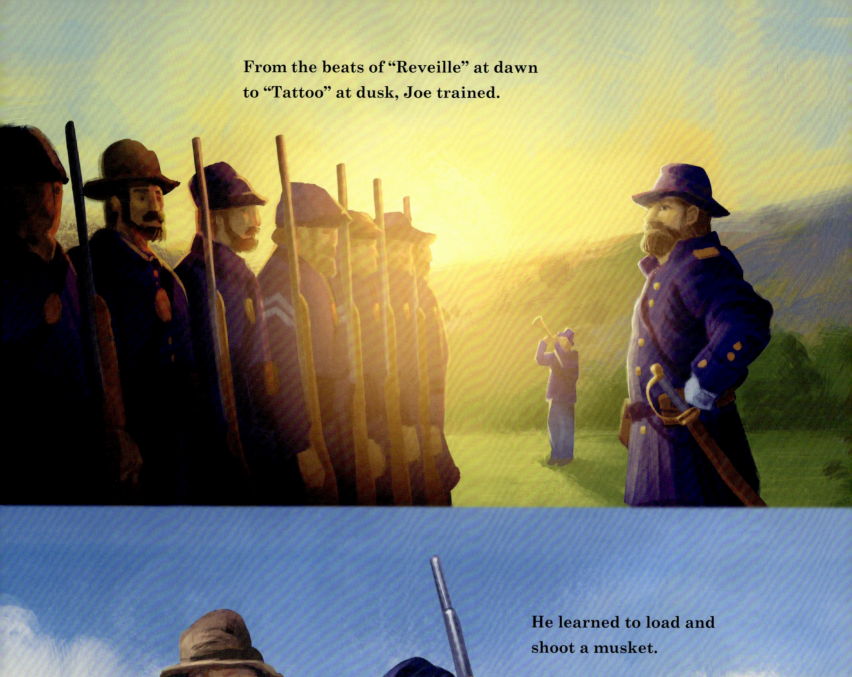

He learned to load and
shoot a musket.

He practiced drills. He memorized drum signals for different maneuvers.

He fell asleep to the lonely lullaby of "Taps."

And he marched. For hundreds of miles,
in blazing sun and drenching rain.

He slept on hard ground, in mud, on rocks.
There was never enough to eat.

Unused to carrying heavy knapsacks, other soldiers fainted in the heat.

Not Joe.

Joe fought in battle after battle.

When other soldiers deserted their posts, Joe stayed.

When other soldiers chose the rear lines,
Joe chose the front.
When other soldiers remained silent,
Joe volunteered.

For his bravery, Joe was promoted to corporal.

At last, the war won,

Joe returned home.

Nine months later, he became a citizen.

He had proved himself as a sailor, a student, a soldier, a man.

But it wasn't enough. Fear and hatred of Chinese people grew among white Americans.

When Joe wanted to marry Martha, no local reverend would help.

Marriage between people of different races was not considered proper.

He and Martha had to travel to Branford, Connecticut,
a day's journey by horse-drawn carriage,

to get married.

Many white Americans blamed the Chinese for the lack of jobs and income.

COME OUT AND RATIFY
Come Everybody!

NO MORE CHINESE

...ratic County of

HIP! HURRAH
CHINESE EXCLUDED

The
Democratic Chinese Exclusion Bill
Has Been Signed by
OUR DEMOCRATIC PRESIDENT

Hip! Hurrah! The White Man is on Top!
DEMOCRAT and all other GOP citi...
...sify this

...CRATIC ME...

Laws were passed prohibiting Chinese people from entering the United States or becoming citizens.

CHINESE? NO! NO! NO!

DOWN WITH THE CHINESE

GIVE OUR BOYS EMPLOYMENT

NO CHINESE!

OUR LAND

THE CHINESE MUST GO!

NO MORE CHINESE EMIGRATION

DOWN WITH THE CHINESE

NO CHINESE CHEAP LABOR FOR US

With pistols and clubs, white people drove Chinese residents out of their homes in violent attacks.

Joe had a wife and children to protect.

With a heavy heart, he cut off the braid he had worn so proudly for years. Shoulders drooping, he told people that he was Japanese, not Chinese, because Japanese people did not face as much discrimination.

Joe had fought hard for freedom, for fair treatment, for his future. He knew he deserved these rights, but now they were being taken away again.

Perhaps for the first time,
Joe wondered if America
was worthy of him.

From captive to corporal to citizen, Joe faced
hardship with courage, integrity, and dignity.

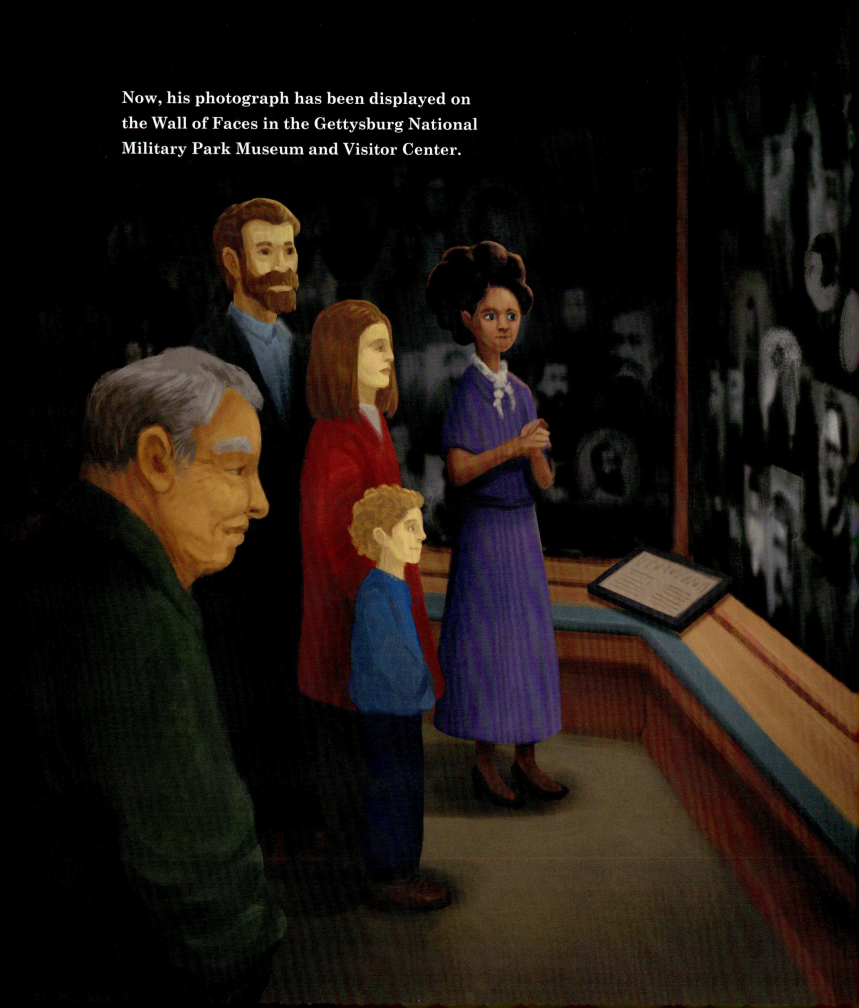

Now, his photograph has been displayed on the Wall of Faces in the Gettysburg National Military Park Museum and Visitor Center.

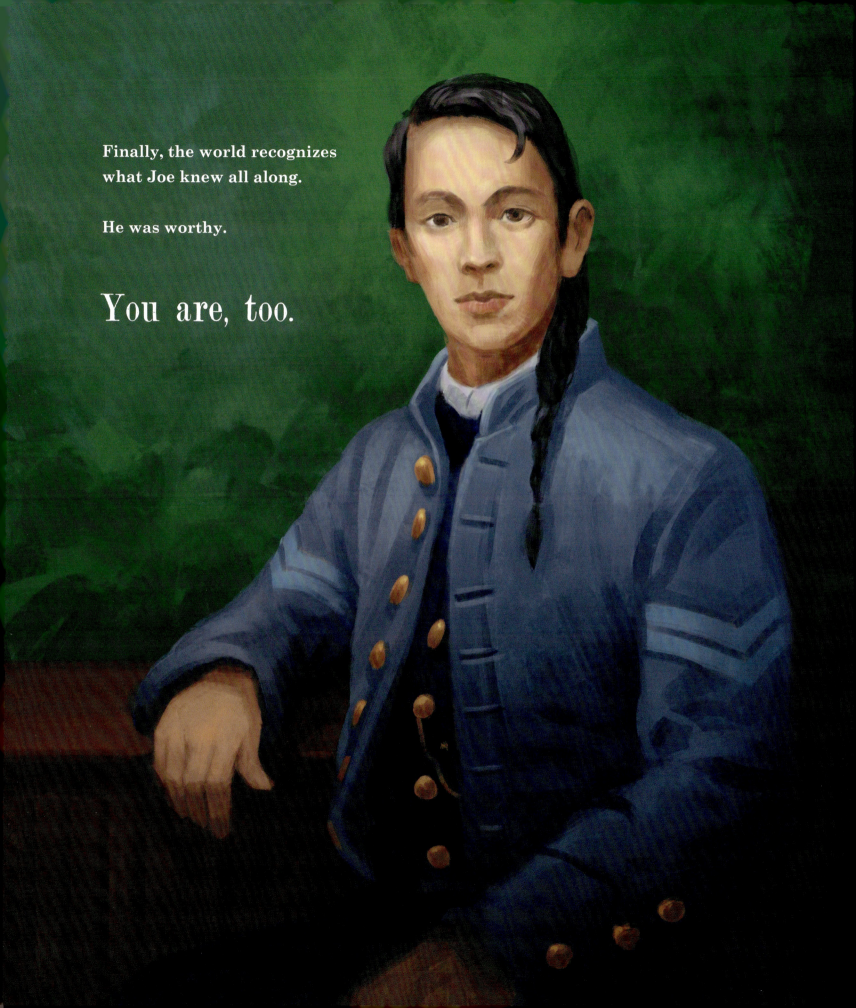

Finally, the world recognizes
what Joe knew all along.

He was worthy.

You are, too.

1861
THE AMERICAN CIVIL WAR BEGINS.

1870
Joe works as a silver engraver, a job he would hold until his retirement.

1842
Joseph Pierce (*birth name unknown*) assumed born in Canton, China (*now known as Guangdong, China*).

1855
Joe assumed sold to Amos Peck, captain of *The Hound*. Later left in the care of the Peck family in Connecticut.

1862
Joe enlists in the 14th Regiment of the Connecticut Volunteer Infantry, Company F.

1876
Joe marries Martha Morgan.

1881
Joe and Martha's second child, Edna Bertha, is stillborn.

1840   1850   1860   1870   1880

1858
Joe's future wife, Martha Morgan, born in Portland, Connecticut.

1863
PRESIDENT LINCOLN SIGNS THE EMANCIPATION PROCLAMATION.

Joe is appointed corporal.

1879
Joe and Martha's first child, Lula Edna, is born.

1882
Joe and Martha's third child, Franklin Norris, is born.

1865
THE CONFEDERATE ARMY SURRENDERS, ENDING THE WAR.

Joe returns to work on the Peck farm in Connecticut.

CONGRESS PASSES THE CHINESE EXCLUSION ACT, WHICH PROHIBITS CHINESE WORKERS FROM IMMIGRATING TO THE UNITED STATES FOR TEN YEARS.

1866
Joe becomes a U.S. citizen, based on his military service.

1884
Joe and Martha's fourth child, Howard Benjamin, is born.

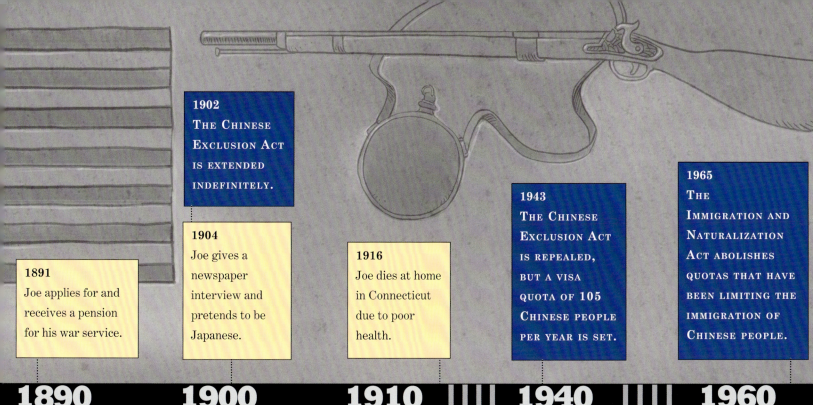

1902
THE CHINESE EXCLUSION ACT IS EXTENDED INDEFINITELY.

1943
THE CHINESE EXCLUSION ACT IS REPEALED, BUT A VISA QUOTA OF 105 CHINESE PEOPLE PER YEAR IS SET.

1965
THE IMMIGRATION AND NATURALIZATION ACT ABOLISHES QUOTAS THAT HAVE BEEN LIMITING THE IMMIGRATION OF CHINESE PEOPLE.

1904
Joe gives a newspaper interview and pretends to be Japanese.

1916
Joe dies at home in Connecticut due to poor health.

1891
Joe applies for and receives a pension for his war service.

1890 **1900** **1910** |||| **1940** |||| **1960**

1892
THE GEARY ACT EXTENDS THE CHINESE EXCLUSION ACT FOR ANOTHER DECADE AND REQUIRES CHINESE PEOPLE TO REGISTER AND CARRY DOCUMENTATION.

Joe refuses to register until forced. Joe also is baptized and becomes a member of Trinity Methodist Episcopal Church.

TIMELINE

Key events in Joe Pierce's life
Historical benchmarks

Author's Note

When my editor suggested that I write a book about the Chinese who fought in the American Civil War, I was stunned. I'd had no idea that any Civil War soldiers were Asian, much less Chinese. Like most people in the United States, I wasn't taught about the people of color who fought in the American Civil War. Their service wasn't deemed worthy of mention and was deliberately left out of textbooks and curriculums. This was not an isolated occurrence—the erasure of people of color from the history of the United States began as soon as white Europeans settled on this continent and continues to this day. The fact is that the United States was built upon the labor and sacrifice of Asian, Black, Brown, and Indigenous people. We owe it to them to recognize and proclaim the important contributions they made (and continue to make) to our country.

Almost nothing remains of Joseph Pierce's possessions. I know of only three items—two photographs of Joe and one of his young daughter. He left behind no personal letters, journals, or documents—at least, none that I or other researchers have found. The exact details of his birth and how he came to be in the possession of Captain Amos Peck may never be known. Other accounts say that Joe was sold by his older brother or was found adrift in the ocean. The version presented in this book is the one I felt was most likely to be true.

In order to write *Worthy*, I relied on primary sources such as military documents, newspaper articles, governmental records, and historical accounts of the 14th Regiment of the Connecticut Volunteer Infantry. Secondary sources, including research, articles, and books by others, were also invaluable. I used the facts of Joe's life, his actions, and society's attitude toward Chinese people at the time to portray what he might have seen, felt, and experienced.

I researched and wrote this book during the pandemic, as anti-Asian hate and violence surged across the country. Just like in Joe's time, Chinese and other Asian Americans and Pacific Islanders are being unfairly blamed for economic and social problems. From March 2020 to March 2022, the Stop AAPI Hate reporting center received 11,467 reports of hate incidents. Just like in Joe's time, newspaper articles, statements by politicians, and other media outlets have been stoking the flames of anti-Asian hate.

The subtitle for this book comes from H. S. Stevens, who was a chaplain in Joe's regiment during the Civil War. In an 1899 article in *The New York Times*, Reverend Stevens said, "The regiment had an exceptional experience as to the number and severity of battles engaged in, hardship of campaigns, and casualties, and 'Our Joe,' as we called him, was rarely off duty—a brave, capable, and faithful soldier." This is the Joe that I wanted readers to see—the Joe who was brave, capable, and faithful, not *in spite of* his race, but because he simply *was* all of these things as a human being.

Acknowledgments

I am deeply indebted to my editor, the brilliant Arthur A. Levine, for alerting me to the presence of Asian American and Pacific Islander soldiers in the Civil War. Not only would this book not exist without him, but I likely would have remained ignorant of this important piece of Asian American history. Thank you, Arthur! I also wish to acknowledge the work of historians Ruthanne Lum McCunn and Irving Moy in shedding light on Joseph Pierce's life. Lastly, thanks to all those who labor to make this country freer and more equitable for everyone, regardless of their race, ethnicity, and religion. Let us all strive to make this country worthy of us.

Select Bibliography

Ancestry.com. *Selected U.S. Naturalization Record Indexes, 1791–1966 (Indexed in World Archives Project)* [online database]. Provo, UT: Ancestry.com Operations, 2010.

Bae, Annie, et al. "The Blame Game: How Political Rhetoric Inflames Anti-Asian Scapegoating." October 2022, https://stopaapihate.org/wp-content/uploads/2022/10/Stop-AAPI-Hate-Scapegoating-Report.pdf.

The Blue, the Gray and the Chinese: American Civil War Participants of Chinese Descent. https://bluegraychinese.blogspot.com.

Connelly, Kevin T. "The 14th Regiment, Connecticut Volunteers, Infantry." USAWC Strategy Research Project. U.S. Army War College, Pennsylvania, 12 January 2000.

Historical Data Systems, comp. *U.S. Civil War Soldier Records and Profiles, 1861–1865* [online database]. Provo, UT: Ancestry.com Operations, 2009.

The Journal. Joseph Pierce obituary. Newspapers.com. 3 January 1916.

Kwok, Gordon. "Association to Commemorate the Chinese Serving in the American Civil War." Association to Commemorate the Chinese Serving in the American Civil War, 18 January 2009. Sites.google.com/site/accsacw/.

Lee, Erika. *The Making of Asian America.* New York: Simon and Schuster, 2015.

"Local Jap Talks: Joseph A. Pierce Thinks Japan Will Win. Says Country is Progressive and Has Strong Army." *The Meriden Weekly Republican.* Newspapers.com, 3 March 1904.

McCunn, Ruthanne Lum. *Chinese Yankee: A True Story from the Civil War.* Design Enterprises of San Francisco, undated.

McCunn, Ruthanne Lum. Personal correspondence, 2020.

Moy, Irving D. *An American Journey: My Father, Lincoln, Joseph Pierce and Me.* Lulu.com, 2010.

Moy, Irving D. "Reflections on the Civil War and Joseph Pierce." 14th Connecticut Volunteer Infantry. www.cof14thcvi.com.

Page, Charles D. *History of the Fourteenth Regiment, Connecticut Volunteer Infantry.* Horton Printing Company, 1906.

Shively, Carol A., ed. *Asians and Pacific Islanders and the Civil War.* Washington DC: National Park Service, 2015.

Stoeckel, Herbert J. "Oriental Yank from Berlin: 100th Anniversary of Battle of Gettysburg Revives the Mystery of Joseph Pierce, Perhaps the Only China Native in Army of Potomac." *The Courant Magazine, Hartford Courant,* 30 June 1963.

Stoeckel, Herbert J. "Tales of Old Hartford: More About the Chinese Yankee." *The Courant Magazine, Hartford Courant,* 4 August 1963 (available at Newspapers.com).

Yellow Horse, Aggie J., et al. "Two Years and Thousands of Voices: What Community-Generated Data Tells Us About Anti-AAPI Hate." July 2022, https://stopaapihate.org/wp-content/uploads/2022/07/Stop-AAPI-Hate-Year-2-Report.pdf.

Citations

Here are the sources for the quotations used in the text, in the order in which they appear.

"The Chinese are ignorant and insolent": "Literary and Critical: Late War and Progress-in-China," *The New York Times,* 2 October 1852.

"They will not work unless treated . . .": "Celestial Immigration," *The New York Times,* 28 May 1855.

"The Chinese of California celebrated May-day . . .": Untitled article, *The Hartford Courant,* 24 August 1855.

"None but parents among a heathen . . .": "Letter from China," *Raleigh Christian Advocate,* 22 December 1859.

"Your Chinaman is the most worthless citizen possible": "Celestial Immigration," *The New York Times,* 28 May 1855.

"not of our people and never will be": Luo, Michael. "The Forgotten History of the Purging of Chinese from America," *The New Yorker.* 22 April 2021.

"One more chance to serve your country…": This reproduction of a recruiting poster for the 14th Regiment can be found at https://members.tripod.com/bliss_barn/livinghistory.html.

"poor sailors and no soldiers at all": "Celestial Immigration," *The New York Times,* 28 May 1855.

"If I can't serve my country as a soldier . . .": "Jos. Pierce, Veteran Soldier: The War Record of a Well Known and Respected Meriden Resident," *The Meriden Journal,* 19 September 1887.

THIS IS AN ARTHUR A. LEVINE BOOK
PUBLISHED BY LEVINE QUERIDO

LQ
LEVINE QUERIDO

www.levinequerido.com • info@levinequerido.com

Levine Querido is distributed by Chronicle Books, LLC

Library of Congress Control Number: 2024950472

ISBN 978-1-64614-557-7

Printed and bound in China

FSC
www.fsc.org

MIX
Paper | Supporting
responsible forestry
FSC™ C008047

Published August 2025

First Printing

Book design by Joy Chu
The text type was set in Century Schoolbook Bold

The art for this book was painted in acrylics on
illustration boards, scanned, and finished digitally
using Escape motions Rebell 6, Autodesk Maya, and
Adobe Photoshop.